Postcards from My Bedroom

Postcards from My Bedroom

JOHN MAMARIL

Paperback: 979-8-9895623-0-5
Hardcover: 979-8-9895623-1-2
Ebook: 979-8-9895623-2-9

Contents

This book is dedicated to my niece:
Eva Kai Dantay

A wonderful life is excited to finally meet you
and the universe is better
simply because
you are in it.

"No matter how obsessed,
you've been with your own
vanishing, there will
always be someone who
wants you whole."

—Hanif Abdurraqib

Postcard from My Bedroom

I live my life so quietly,
sometimes I wonder
if I even exist at all.

I have always been better
at holding hands
than conversations
and more comfortable
in cardigans
than I have ever been
in crowds.

My footsteps whisper apologies
to the ground
for being a disturbance,
my bed questions
my excuses for leaving,
and the day always asks night
if I will ever see her again.

My ego is a minor character
with no lines
in an unpopular play
in the emptiest theater.

I am the quietest silhouette
in the background
of everybody else's lives
and no one ever asks
if the backdrop gets stage fright.

How nice it would be
to be noticed.

Amateur

As an artist
I take comfort in the fact
that even though I hold my guitar
like it was a mistake how it got there,

that when my fingers somehow
fumble their way into
the shape of a C chord,

and my hand strums
with absolutely no confidence,
as if it just figured out
how to move on its own –

the noise that is made
is still considered music
and a sound is grateful
to be heard.

The Moulting

There are not many days
when I decide to compare myself
to a crab
but sometimes
people make you feel
like a crustacean.

When you are thirty-five pounds more
than what everyone expects you to be,
it is difficult to believe that
you still have some growing to do.

That is when happens when you mix
depression with dysmorphia.

It is hoping that your eyes and the mirror
aren't magnetic to all the parts of yourself
you don't love –
which is every part.

It is questioning all the compliments
and none of the criticisms.

It is loving the different body
but maybe still not the person
inside of it.

People like to think
any transformation
is a metamorphosis
but they do not understand
a moulting
is what you must go through
to grow
and
all of it is ugly.

Lessons from Empaths

Attention is the
purest form
of generosity
and kindness
is always loud
even if it is just
a whispered encouragement
or soft eye contact
or a silent smile.

Doomed

Dear Fate,

I was just wondering
if happiness is in my stars
because lately it just feels like
you haven't been on my side
and honestly
it feels like you have never been
in the first place
and I was kind of hoping
that maybe you could start
sometime soon.

I heard you have a busy schedule
and I was hoping maybe you could
please just donate
two seconds of your time
because it seems like everyone else
is dining on sunshine and wine
and all I am asking for is
a taste.

I know lightning never hits
the same place twice
so I have no idea why I hoped
the same law would apply
to rejection.

I guess I kind of
opened myself up
for this one.

Behind

At this age,
my accomplishments
question if
they are even real
and
expectations are new people
I am finding
harder and harder
to meet.

Distant

Did you know
that space is so vast
that in a billion years
when the Andromeda
and Milky Way galaxies
finally make their spectacular collision,
not a single star will touch one another?

That is how vast space is.

That is how far

I feel I am

From other people.

Invertebrate

My first date
was at the San Diego Zoo.

As we entered the bug exhibit
brightly colored stands
guarded the entrance
like warning signs
with the words
"mysterious" "creepy" "interesting"

The girl I was with
let out a laugh
as she pointed out
they were all words
that described me.

I read in one of the infographics
there is an insect called
the dead leaf butterfly.

I often imagine why
people like me walk around
pretending we are meant to fall
when we were born to fly.

In nature,
they call it camouflage.

I just call it my depression.

So here I am today -
afraid of cameras
and intimate moments.

This is close as I can get to a self-portrait.

Here I am, some boy
who puts on poetry
as a mask every morning
because isn't that what it is?
Just a makeshift concealer
to hide the blemishes
I call my own malfunctions.

I've learned that camouflage
is less one of my self-defense mechanisms
and more my natural skin.
If you took a kaleidoscope
to my soul, you would only see
every spectrum of the gray scale
and how much it weighs me down
to exist as my own illusion -
even shadows
want to grow up
to be silhouettes someday.

I want to be a ghost
in more ways than one -
not the kind
who disappears on Tinder
or wears white sheets,
but just something more tangible
than the figment I already am.

To be felt.

I am just so tired
all of the time.

How can not existing
be this exhausting?

I feel as if
I am not even

here.

II

Surf Lessons

The ocean
is a jealous lover;
it will happily accept
all of your crashes
before it ever
lets you
kiss the sky.

Oleander

In the aftermath of
the atomic bombing
of Hiroshima
all that remained
from the firestorm
was dusty gray
and scorched rubble.

The radiation levels were believed
to be so high
nothing could ever possibly grow again
and now
radiation exposure is
associated with unnatural mutations,
Godzilla,
cancer and x-rays,
or a superhero's origin story.

But the interesting part of this catastrophe
is that despite being seeded
in the soil of devastation,
a plant called oleander
decided it would be the first living thing
to bloom from ashes—

Which is to say
there is always the chance of
growth after disaster;
even if it just flickers
even if it just flashes.

"Come Closure"

In August of 2008,
R&B artist Ne-Yo
releases his single "Closer"
much to the delight
of bodies in nightclubs
everywhere.

Relevant but unrelated,
I experience my first break-up
three years later.

In an attempt to cheer me up,
my cousins bring me
to the loudest district
in downtown San Diego
and it is like
the entire skyline
has come to party.

The lights are flashing to the beat,
being still is grounds
for a ticket and a fine,
even the skyscrapers
seem to stretch like they are
putting their hands up.

Surrounded by hips telling the truth
and the aftermath of my ex lying -
I have become someone
who has cried in the club.

Still,
I chose to dance
because even though
I misunderstood the lyrics,
my body can't help
but have a conversation
with the music.

Reverence

Years from now,

when even free throws
have become costly
to my body
and overtime means
staying up past 8pm,

when my knees
beg the referees for more timeouts
and my joints develop amnesia
on the definition of fastbreaks,

when the only ankle breakers I cause
are to myself
and I feel my past opponent's terror
of helplessly watching my body
as it fades away,

I will still crumple up paper trash
and shape them into uneven globes -
pretend to dribble, pump fake,
and turn over my shoulder -
set my feet, leap, follow through,
and loft my shot to the heavens
the way you used to.

"Kobe."

Today,
these will not be
the first
or
the last
prayers I send up
with your name.

Asian Parents

My accomplishments
are a home cooked meal -
one my mother
can only force two spoonfuls
of disappointment
before pushing her plate away
and claiming that
she is not hungry.

Pluto is a Planet (For Solomon)

When the science museum
put eight planets on display
instead of nine,
the astrophysicist Neil DeGrasse Tyson
received what I can only imagine
is the first incident of hate mail
addressed to a scientist
from a child.

Perhaps,
being experts themselves in
knowing what it is like
to be stripped
of deserved standing and significance
for the crime
of being "too small,"
children all over the world
sent countless letters
to address the injustice
against their beloved planet.

*"You are going to have to take all of the books away and
change them!"*

*"Do people live on Pluto? If there are people who live
there they won't exist."*

*"Some people like Pluto. If it doesn't exist then they
don't have a favorite planet. Please write back but not in
cursive because I can't read in cursive."*

*"Remember all of those kids that sent you bad letters?
We're sorry about giving you mean letters saying we love
Pluto but not you."*

What I admire most
is that despite
their lack of eloquence
and abundance of misspellings,
they believed so strongly about
the planet Pluto
something in their little bones
told them to tell
the scientist who spent his entire career
being right
that he was absolutely wrong.

I cannot wait
until they find out
about gravity.

Who would dare to be brave enough
to tell these children
that they cannot fly?

Equations

Awkward = Smooth - Smooth

Picture = Word x 1000

Math = Numbers + Letters + Massive Confusion

Music = Sound x Soul

Coffee = Drink of the gods + 6:00 AM

Secret = (Confession)

Motivation = Food

Crush = Person of Interest + Distance^{10}

My Head (Sometimes) = Balloon - String

Best Friend = Friend - Other Friends

Boy = Human + Stupid^2

Gentleman = Boy + Manners

Valentine's Day = (Average day + Gifts) - Money

Cupid = (Angel + Bow) - Good Aim

Fairy Tale = Life + Happily Ever After

Regret = (Decision + Fun)/Time

Success = What You Love/What You Do

Love = (Like x Like)^{1,000,000}

Oxymoron

Is it possible to be a stranger to yourself?

I feel like I am
a multitude of everything
and a compilation
of nothing.

I just want to figure out
if I am a paradox
or a walking antonym.
I am still learning to see
which box
I actually fit in.

Maybe I am just an oxymoron.

I have always felt like my
only option
to fit in was to
act natural
but I have never felt like I am
one whole piece,
always more like
an original copy.

But what else is new?

I am Asian-American.

I am Filipino
but apparently
sometimes Chinese
or Korean.

What difference does it make
since we all look like?

How else can we be the "Kung Flu"
but if we get your temperature high enough
you just tested positive for yellow fever?
Either way, we are the cause
of your illness.

In America,
we make up 17.1% of the doctors
and one hundred percent of the problems.
We exist as both the antidote, the cure,
but mostly the virus.
We are the relief, the remedy,
the target of retaliation.
We are both the comfort and the threat.
We are trespassers with passports.
We are the mystical martial artists
and we are the elderly punching bags.
We have always been the silhouettes
and now we are chalk outlines.

When I read about the shooting
at the massage spa in Atlanta,
in the midst of trying to understand
the aftermath,
I asked myself
"Didn't they read the brochure?"

A massage is only meant to relax the body,
to make the blood and oxygen
within
remember what it feels like
to flow.

To feel free from pain.

I don't know if I will ever know what that is like,
I do know that is all I ever want us to be.

For Asian-Americans
we have always been
two things at once.

I ache for the day where
we are neither
the blame
nor the victims.

Magicians (For my Mother Mariagida)

There is a theory
that when women become mothers,
they also become magicians.

The way their hands
already know where to be
to catch you
when your body
decides to turn its own clumsiness
into a collision.

The way they can make
a FaceTime celebration
feel as if
they are right there
in the stands.

How anytime you need them
to back you up -
there they are:
somehow
standing both beside
and in front of you.

My mom is living proof
mothers are the only beings
who have mastered
the secret art of being
in two places
at once.

First Date

It is 2011 and I am in the Skyfari
at the San Diego Zoo
staring into the eyes of the girl
who I would forever associate
the word "dazzling" with.

I'm sitting there wearing
a black cashmere sweater
in July of all months and she is
looking back at me
like I mean something,
like I am not some seventeen-year-old boy
masquerading as a guy
who knows exactly what he is doing
(and isn't afraid of heights).

We are sitting there quietly
and I'm thinking a lot of things;
like if it is scientifically possible for plants
to photosynthesize from someone's smile
and if I was her first choice
and if I wasn't then
was I her last one
and was I the right one
(I wasn't)

and if I wasn't would she be the girl
I'd look for in crowded areas
and places she would never be
(she was)

and if we were Amazon products
would we be recommended for
purchasing together
and would her reviews
be better than mine
(probably)

and how I wish she would stop
staring at me like I'm a pot of gold
at the end of a rainbow
when I'm just a plastic red cup
full of pennies
(she didn't).

I just kept wondering
if I had the chance to
look into her soul
would it feel like
I was in the third grade
looking into a kaleidoscope
for the first time

and how even though her smile
was weighed down by a past
it still manages to reach her eyes
and how she makes me want to
tell her all my secrets
when I am the kind of guy
who looks for an escape hatch
in every single conversation
I find myself in

and how most people
are just ripples in my life
and she was a tsunami.

Finally, I stop thinking
and I just look at her
and the sun is setting
in the background
and the light is hitting her hair
in all the right places

and I am reminded of this line
that F. Scott Fitzgerald wrote in
The Beautiful and Damned
about a girl who was
dazzling and alight
and that it was agony
to comprehend her beauty
in a glance
and he was so right
and the English language is beautiful
and so was she.

He was so right.

So was she.

Procrastination

I wonder
if there are stations
where you can refuel
your motivation
because I have
a five-minute tank
that I just filled up
and somehow
it is already
empty.

Romantics Like
(After Andrew Simmons)

Romantics like slow dancing. Romantics like
saxophone instrumentals. Romantics like infinitesimal
possibilities. Romantics like admiring from afar.
Romantics like crying and rocky road ice cream.
Romantics like Disney movies. Romantics like to
swoon and sigh. Romantics like rooftops and city
lights. Romantics like kissing in the rain even though
it is really uncomfortable. Romantics like being weak
in the knees. Romantics like Daniel Caesar songs.
Romantics like anticipation.

Romantics like listening to good poetry and then writing
bad poems. Romantics like holding hands. Romantics
like Titanic and The Notebook. Romantics like being
clingy. Romantics like the stars, the seas, and other
cosmic occurrences. Romantics like quotes, like really
really really like quotes. Romantics like to search for
shooting stars even in the cloudiest of skies. Romantics
like clichés. Romantics like marriage proposals.
Romantics like crying at the thought of their own
marriage proposals. Romantics like magic carpet rides.

Romantics like first kisses. Romantics like having crushes. Romantics like drive-in theaters. Romantics like to think long-distance relationships are cute. (Romantics are wrong.) Romantics like happily ever afters. Romantics like to chicken out when they are about to take a risk. Romantics like second-guessing. Romantics like gloomy mornings and rainy afternoons. Romantics like stories about a vampire and a werewolf fighting for a human's love. Romantics like blankets and pillow forts. Romantics like Paris.

Romantics like Ferris wheels, sharing cotton candy, and winning giant teddy bears at the fair. Romantics like candle lit dinners and rose petal sheets. Romantics like cozy fireplaces. Romantics like Airbnbs. Romantics like to wander the Valentine's Day aisle and promise not to buy anything. Romantics like forehead kisses. Romantics like hands on their waist. Romantics like reunions. Romantics like dreaming and telling any human that appears in them to hurry the hell up. Romantics like long walks on Honeymoon Avenue. Romantics like secrets.

Romantics like Netflix. Romantics like to Google synonyms for the word "beautiful". Romantics like mixing math with love and thinking it's the cutest damn thing ever. Romantics like dessert. Romantics like to cry to "Little Things" by One Direction. Romantics like daydreaming. Romantics like poems that start with roses are red and violets are blue. Romantics like to believe in magic. Romantics like to listen to Rudy Francisco so much they start speaking in metaphors and similes. Romantics like compliments and reassurances. Romantics like melting.

Romantics like Pinterest. Romantics like planning their wedding ten years in advance. Romantics like Hawaii. Romantics like small gestures. Romantics like to know other people's Love Language. Romantics like good morning texts and good night kisses and sometimes switching them around. Romantics like surprises. Romantics like making mix tapes. Romantics like stealing hoodies and jackets. Romantics like the idea of falling in love in one day. Romantics like getting carried away.

Romantics like PDA but not too much P with the DA. Romantics like happy endings. Romantics like to compare real life interests to fictional characters. Romantics like OTPs and shipping. Romantics like staying in and drinking red wine. Romantics like to believe in miracles. Romantics like singing Boyz II Men songs in the shower. Romantics like flowers and chocolates. Romantics like to have celebrity crushes. Romantics like to be cuddled more than they like cuddling. Romantics like Disneyland.

Most of all, romantics love to put the hopeless in hopeless romantic.

An Angel You've Always Been
(For JJ Dantay)

When you arrived to *Heaven*,
all of God's angels lined up
to meet you with a warm embrace.
They said, "Well, if isn't JJ!"
and welcomed you back home
to those golden gates.

They blessed you
with all kinds of questions:
like, how was your journey
and did you learn from your mistakes,
did you always give your best and
if you ever found love or just heartbreaks?

They replayed the best moments of your life
and told you about their favorite parts:
like the proudest you ever made your father feel
and the first time your mother held you in her arms,
every single laugh you shared with your big sister,
every single time your brother protected you from harm.

In all of those memories,
your smile is so radiant
it made everyone around you
glow and glimmer;
your smile is so bright
even the stars were jealous of the way
you made everything shimmer.

When the angels beckoned
that it was finally time to go —
to forever leave this earthly garden
and wander that everlasting orchard —
every part of you wanted to fall back down
instead of ascending forward.

And your only thoughts were about
all of the tomorrows that would start without you,
all of the yesterdays you will forever exist in,
all of the people you would be leaving behind —
and how you wish
you could have stayed
and how you wish
you could have had more time.

But when the angels saw
how sad you lamented
and how you wished
that your loved ones
could come along,
you felt a hand on your shoulder
that pulled you in for a hug
and God said,

"JJ, my son, Heaven
is also every moment we have
with the people that we love."

III

Love Letter from the Dictionary to
the Thesaurus

I love how
you take the words
right out of my pages
and rearrange
all of me
to show I can be
something beautiful
outside of my own
definition.

Love Letter from My Hands to Your Hips

You are my favorite distraction.

The one that reminds me that I am more
than creaky knuckles and a wrinkled palm,
always feeling brittle and clenched.

You give me the kind of amnesia
that makes my fingers forget
how to form a fist.
You teach them that it is okay
to be unfurled
and open to the world
especially when you are the one
filling that space.

I would be lying if I said that
I am never nervous
before any audition
to play the role of your applause
or when I ask your curves
to etch their autograph
into my fingertips.

I know how selfish it is
to ask for a piece of your warm horizon,
of the arch I keep wanting to melt into.
I feel like that is why you laugh at me
whenever we get into arguments
over letting go too soon.

I suppose I am just tired
of standing here
pretending I am not hovering
from your gravity,
that I am not stealing moments
to linger in your orbit.

But your touch always gives my fingers
the kind of voltage
that leaves them silently hoping
for a chance
at another graze.

Love Letter to the COVID-19 Quarantine

I can only imagine
what it is like to be
what is best for someone
and still not be wanted,
to not be listened to,
to be the friend
everybody needs to talk to
once in a while
but no one wants to visit.

I hope that
whenever you read
another Facebook post of
"How can I make this about me?"
that you realize that you are:

the soft rain
everybody complains about
getting them wet and
no one wants to stand in,
the kind of light
that sends everybody
rushing for shade,
the gentle storm
that continues
to water the flowers
even if we
are not thankful
for being given
the chance to grow.

When this is over,
we will realize
that you were the fresh air
we needed
and the reason why
after you are gone
we are still alive
to breathe.

Love Letter from the Wet Floor Sign to the Ceiling Fan

You are the centerpiece
of all furniture that are
designed to adorn
higher altitudes.

The way you float above clocks
who cling to the days
when their tick tocks
got more attention
and hover over all the
lopsided photo frames
dangling beneath you.

The way you rotate
to create the gentlest hurricanes
and infuse every room
with the breeze
of your quiet carousel.

You would be any architect's
favorite airborne ornament.

I know that I am unremarkable
how I am so low and stationary,
how I am not to be noticed
except to be a notice for others,
how I exist only to be avoided.

I hope that if I am ever part of an
unexpected renovation,
or if I am ever moved
to another forgotten corridor,
or if I am chosen to guard another spill -
I hope your flow still finds me.

But while we are both still here
if you ever get bored of your own orbit -
wouldn't it be a remarkable thing
if I could join you sometime?

I promise if there is one thing
I am good at -
it will be
not letting you
slip by.

Love Letter from the Traveler to the Destination

Sometimes,
when I am craving you -
I pretend that all cartographers
are bad at their jobs.

I like to imagine
that globes are the wrong kind of shape,
that atlases lost a fight to encyclopedias,
that charts of the world
are backwards
and upside down.

I want to crinkle
every single map I see
until California
kisses your location
like how I want you
to kiss me.

I want to act like
the only thing correct
about time zones
is that you are somewhere
in my future.

I know that I am being silly,
blaming map makers
for our physical distance
as much as I blame cancelled flights,
or high-priced airfare,
or the size of all the
oceans and continents
between us.

But I also know that
there is only one kind
of body language
that can touch you
even through a screen,
and intimacy is just our eyes
sending postcards
to one another
so I can see
what you see.

Love Letter to the Red Flag

I do not care
if your love language
is ignoring my texts
and
I will never ask for a refund
for all of my time
that you waste.

I do not mind
that you make pride
seem humble
with all the grudges
you hold in
trophy cases.

I can look past all the petty
behind the pretty
and forget all the warnings
by the morning.

I could not care less
how mean or rude
you can be
because truthfully
you could be any hue
and I would enjoy the view.

So
when people ask me
what I mean,
I just say
that you are
my favorite shade
of green.

Love Letter from the Cosmologist

I read somewhere
that there is a mountain
in Alaska that resembles
a slumbering woman.

Sometimes,
I too wonder
how you were carved
from the cosmos.

The way you make constellations look like
first grade drawings
that never made it to the refrigerator,
how it seems like the auroras
are always competing in contests
to be your shadow.
I imagine you make the horizon
feel uneven
and jealous of your curves.
Even the sunrise
feels gray around you
and the moon questions
if it is half as bright.

I just know that you make me
so nervous,
my hands tremble like an eleven
on the Richter scale.
I have to remind them
that the tsunami warnings
are false alarms
when they decide to be
sweatier than usual.
I do all I can
to stop myself from becoming
a natural disaster
in your presence.

I have no idea
if you came from the cosmos
but I bet your lips
feel like the waves
and
taste like the stars.

My favorite part
is how you could just stand still
and give everyone
a show.

Love Letter from Michelangelo to Medusa

I tirelessly
etch and chisel
to turn marble
into marvels
while you effortlessly
create beauty
in all you see –
do you get
why it is impossible
not to turn to stone
when I catch
you looking
at me?

Love Letter from the Question Mark to the Comma

You are the life of the party
when it comes to punctuation.

I imagine apostrophes are envious of
how grounded you are,
you make dashes and colons
feel jealous and unemployed,
quotation marks
will always show up
if you show up,
and everybody loves seeing you
in their bank accounts.

Can you imagine how wonderful you are?
I mean that with no asterisks.
To juggle three things at once,
to not know where to place you,
and you never have to end.

I love watching you move.
The way you can just keep
going,
and going,
and going,
and going.

What I love the most
is how you let everyone know
that it's okay to pause sometimes,
to just take a breath
every once in a while.

I would never keep you a secret in parenthesis,
never let a hyphen come between us,
never let a period take my place.
The only brackets for me
are the ones where you are the champion.

I say this despite my habit
of being uncertain,
and second guessing myself.
I always feel like I have come to an end
and everybody already knows where I belong.

I am the wallflower of the English language.
I am never the first to enter a room
or to be the center of attention.
You will never fail to find me
lurking near the exit
or by myself.

I have a stem with no petals
that curves like it cannot decide
which direction to wilt
and a root so disconnected
I wonder how I can
always be stuck in one place.

And then you remind me
that wallflowers are
one of the only plants
that can blossom
in dark corners;

That just by existing,
I too make it easier
for things to breathe;

That just one of me
can be called a bouquet
because you say I am
at the same time
enough
and more.

How lucky I am
that the life of the party
does not mind coming
to my corner.

Love Letter from a Boy to The Girl

The moment you floated into my life
my smile was so eager
to meet yours,
it introduced itself
from the other side of the room
before I could even say
hello.

My eyes shyly made their way
across to yours and asked
if they knew how to play tag
and ever since
it has felt like neither of them
wanted to stop being
"It."

After an afternoon
of subtle glances
and stolen glimpses,
after all of
the playful peeks
and unspoken gazes -
they grew accustomed
to always having you
somewhere within my vision.

Now,
they question any time
you are missing from my sight.

The last time I searched for you,
you waved so softly
as if you had been
waiting for me
to find you
all over again.

Your smile
was like watching
a constellation appear
in high definition.

Your voice
was a mosaic of
all the sounds
that belong to places
my hearing
would have liked to call
home.

Your waist
felt like the treasure
my hand had been
trying to discover
for its entire life.

One day,
I will stand in front of
something remarkable
and someone will ask me
if there could possibly be
a better view
and I'll tell them
they have no idea
while I stare at
what's in front of me
and only think of
you.

IV

Calendars

You have
spring in your step
and an
entire summer
in your smile
but I have
calendars of reasons
why we did not last
two seasons.

Burning

When I hear somebody say,
"You don't look depressed to me."

My mind always fumbles through
some soundtrack of makeshift reasons
I have already prepared for their comfort -
before deciding to just play
everyone's favorite song,
"I know, but it's hard to explain."

Except it isn't.
It's just a lot easier to say than:

I wonder if the sun still gets nervous—
if he has to swallow a gulp,
hide behind the curtain,
and check his watch to see
if enough ticks have passed
until rise becomes set;

all before he has to go back on stage
and perform for those
already accustomed to his light –
for people who believe
that their applause
will somehow allow him
to feel his own warmth.

Innocence

Forgiveness
is every child's
native tongue
and a language
their parents
never bothered
to speak.

Dysmorphia

Most days,
I do not love my body -
the way it always has to find
self-worth in this mismatch
of flesh and veins,
how it manages to make
my blood flow
trickle like it is offbeat,
and can manifest bruises
from intangible thoughts.

When I look in the mirror,
I see this non-certified professional
who dissects my figure
without my permission,
diagnoses my insecurities
as if they were qualified opinions,
and prescribes me discouragement
to numb the pain.

All I see is a stranger
who has grown too comfortable
amputating all of the parts of myself
I want to love;
when I try
to rearrange my figure
into something I can find pride in
I still feel as if I am attempting
self-assembly without instructions.

I hate feeling like
all I am is just
loose bolts
and duct tape.

"Just Friends"

The only thing
foggier than
our understanding
of each other
of each other
is the windows.

Filler
(After Gabe Bondoc)

If all I am is
just missed calls
and ignored notifications
and a cluster
of read receipts

If all I am is
someone who gets jealous
of honorable mentions
and being the guy you meet
before you meet the guy

If all I am is
both the exhilaration
and the disaster,
both the test drive
and the crash dummy

If all I am is
the half-lit neon exit sign
on your way out
from being your entertainment

If all I am is
something that only exists
between when the sun sleeps
and the morning rises

If this is all I am
to you
then I pretend
that is all you are
to me.

Seductive

Your love
dresses up as manipulation,
puts on imitation as a costume
zipped all the way up,
perfumes itself with the scent
of infatuation,
and pretends
it is not the same
as a lie.

Drizzle

Are we ever
going to be more
than two raindrops
who can't touch
without losing themselves
inside of
one another?

Beggar

Believe me
I am not someone
who is hungry
for attention.

You will never catch me
thirsty for praise
or starving to be noticed
or craving a compliment.

But here I am
hoping for yours –

even if it means
the scraps,

even if it means
the crumbs.

V

Curves

I have tried to calculate metaphors
involving geometry
and your skin
like the slope of your back
or the curve of your hips
or the lines of your thighs

but I was never good at
finding answers to
these kinds of things
like proving equations
or figuring us out

so I apologize
if I make mistakes
but this I know
to be true:

there is more than one
right answer
when it comes to
touching you.

Aches

Fact:
it is also possible
to be allergic to
the absence of something.

Crush

People have always
wondered about the unknown
like the cosmos
or
the bottom of
the seven seas
but the only thing
I have ever wondered
is if you
have ever wondered
about me.

Spectrum

Everything with you
is vivid.
It is a privilege
to be in the backdrop
of your light.
Your aura holds the secret
to every sunset.
You remind me
of every tie-dye sunrise.
Even the darkest nights
emit the most dazzling haze.
If I asked to see
the prism of your soul -
would you give me permission?
Or just set me ablaze.
What a beautiful way to glow.

Daylight Savings Time

The sun gets to stay up
past its bedtime
and the morning
sleeps in until noon
but what is losing an hour
to me
if it means more light
with you?

Goddess

I won't pretend
to be some expert
at Greek mythology
but I do know that
Atlas was cursed
to cradle the sky
and after Pegasus died
he was reborn
as the brightest star
and that somewhere on
Mount Olympus
you are making
Aphrodite
incredibly jealous.

Priority

Believe me when I say
that you are never
in the back of my mind -
I have a stream of ideas
patiently waiting
to become thoughts
and all of them know
to move aside
because you belong
at the front
of the line.

Radiant

You have
the kind of smile
that makes the sun
look like
it is flickering.

Migraine

The first time you apologized
for a small mistake
by referring to yourself
as a headache

I laughed
because when I have those
sometimes the pain is so severe
I want to be
as far away from my head
as possible

and that is the exact opposite
of where I want to be
from you.

Crescent

When I say
that I am
crazy for her,
I mean that
if she is the moon
then I am
an absolute lunatic.

Playing It Cool

I would like for you to know
that there is
no such thing
as playing it cool
when you are around me.

My body sabotages itself
like that moment
is the perfect time
to malfunction.

It is like every part of me
decides to get into
their own kind
of silly mischief -

My smile unshackles
itself from its confines
so it can be
the first part of myself
to disobey

My eyes become
the world's worst thieves
hoping you'll catch them
in the act of
stealing glances
at you

My cheeks delude themselves
into pretending like
red is just an undiscovered tone
of camouflage

Even my knees attempt to go undercover
in a discount store disguise
and act like their rattling
isn't giving them away

And if you were to
put my hands in a line-up,
they would be the only suspects
drenched in sweat.

It is like they try every alias,
offer any bribe,
and pay any ransom
just so they do not have to
settle down
when I am around you.

So, whenever it is time
to play it cool
just know that
every part of me
is trying to
break the rules.

Cosmos
(After Ann Druyan)

When I tell people
that I am lucky
when it comes to you,
I don't mean
back-to-back royal flushes
or a bouquet of four-leaf clovers
or even eighteen holes-in-one.

I mean when I think
of the billions of years
you and I could have existed,
then the few
we have together
no longer seem
so small
and fleeting.

I will not waste a moment.
Even one second is plenty of time
to be called yours
and you mine.

How lucky I am
to exist
when you exist.

Dazzling

You are the
kind of beautiful
that gets
everybody's hearts racing
and I always hope
mine is the one
in first place.

Infinite

When I say
I want to live
in this moment with you
I don't mean
to capture it in a photo -
I mean I want to remove the sand
from a million hourglasses
and dump them on the shore
and it could be just you, me,
and sandcastles
endlessly by the sea.

Sunkissed

On mornings
when the sun
decides to call in sick,
I can always smell
its light
in your fragrance.

More Alternatives to the Word "Bae"
(After Rudy Francisco)

The girl who reminds me of
all the best parts in a movie,
who never makes me want to press pause,
the blooper reel -
the one I want to laugh about mistakes with
until we get it right,
the gentlest roller coaster,
the one that makes me the right kind of dizzy,
the high that I never have to chase,
my favorite notification,
the one I always hope
pops up on my lock screen,
the reminder,
the one that gets me through the bad days,
the part that turns them into good ones,
the best part.

VI

Postcard from the Metaphor

Listen,

You cannot keep coming to me
crinkled treasure map in hand
every time
you need to find meaning
in your own life.

Sidestepping things
will not help you
move forward.

If you really want to call yourself
a poet –

Get out of your bedroom.

Let's reimagine the world.

Notes

Postcard from My Bedroom

This poem leads off the collection because when I spent uncountable hours in my room, it was always the one I imagined as a tiny note slipping out beneath the doorway to let the world know I was still here. This book exists because of the most honest poem I have ever written about myself.

The Moulting

This poem addresses the constant conflict I felt with my bodily changes over the years and was an honest attempt at confronting my self-image with self-love. It is still a struggle, but I am grateful for the people in my life who have helped me grow, even those who were not very nice about it.

Lessons From Empaths

This poem is inspired by my friend Samantha – the greatest empath I have ever known. I steal all my secrets to being the best kind of person from her.

Surf Lessons

This poem was written in 2018 and inspired by the winter my cousin and I spent in Huntington Beach countlessly crashing into the Pacific Ocean so that we could float above its waves just once.

Reverence

This poem uses basketball terminology for wordplay. A free throw is an undefended shot at the basket after a foul. A fastbreak is a quick push ahead of the defense to attempt to score quickly. An ankle breaker is a move also known as a crossover used to freeze an opponent in place in order to get around them. The crumpled up paper globes reference the common act of people who mimic a basketball shot into trashcans.

Pluto is a Planet

This poem is inspired by the humorous demotion of Pluto and the love it received from its tiny defenders. Neil deGrasse Tyson still insists Pluto "had it coming" and the unintended ice cold and menacing tone towards a planetary object never fails to make me laugh – just like my nephew Solomon West Torres.

Equations

This poem was a writing exercise from 2012 and remains one of my favorite methods of composing figurative language. Forming a metaphor or simile is not unlike creating an equation. I have an endless appreciation for when mathematics meets poetry.

Oxymoron

This poem was written in the aftermath of the COVID-19 pandemic which saw increased violence against Asian-Americans. I wrote this the day of the August 2021 massage spa shootings.

First Date

This poem was originally a stream of consciousness free write. The date this poem is about is the same one referenced in the piece Invertebrate.

Romantics Like (after Andrew Simmons)

This poem is directly inspired by and in the style of Andrew Simmons' "Ninth Graders Like" that was written in 2013. I adore the repetitive style that combines humor and meticulousness to deliver an accurate description of an entire group. The first draft of this piece was initially "Hopeless Romantics Like" but was changed due to having an excessive number of syllables to pronounce.

An Angel You've Always Been (For JJ Dantay)

I was asked by JJ's family if I would write a poem and read it at his memorial ceremony. It was, of course, an honor but I did have difficulty writing something so emotional that was of a different style and for a different audience. Every word I wrote felt like the wrong one to the point that I was going to instead read a poem by someone else until his brother Joseph told me to just write something from my heart. That is what I did, and I hope this poem helped comfort not only myself but JJ, his family, and everyone who loved him.

Love Letter from the Wet Floor Sign to the Ceiling Fan

This poem is inspired by Sarah Kay's "The Toothbrush to the Bicycle Tire" from No Matter the Wreckage. The challenge to creatively develop and find romance in everyday objects with no relationship to one another is one I enjoy practicing. After watching her performance of this piece on YouTube, I knew at that moment I wanted to aspire to her level of poetic talent.

Love Letter from the Cosmologist

This poem was originally written in 2012 with the title "Star-crossed" and it was incredibly cheesy. It became the love letter form it is today after I stumbled upon an image of the Sleeping Lady mountain formation. What was believed to be Mt. Susitna was actually a computer-generated image and while the photo was edited the feelings that it inspired were not.

Love Letter from the Question Mark to the Comma
This poem was written because a girl asked me, "If you could be any kind of punctuation mark, what would you be?" and while I did not have an answer at the time – the question and the girl both had me feeling some type of way. It is inspired by two people: my favorite friend Triveshni Sharma who is the definition of life of the party and my longtime friend Emma Sadlowski who wrote her song called "Your Wallflower Friend" in 2014.

Love Letter from a Boy to The Girl
This poem was initially titled "For ED" before being changed to "Stuck in the Moment" before finally becoming the last of the Love Letters. It is also the last poem I wrote for this collection.

Filler (After Gabe Bondoc)
This poem was inspired by my favorite musician Gabe Bondoc and his Khalid-inspired song also titled "Filler."

Aches/Crush
These poems were part of a larger piece titled "Words for Every Girl I Had Feelings For" which has since been divided into separate smaller pieces.

Spectrum

This poem was originally going to lead the collection as well as be the namesake for the book.

Goddess

This poem was also a part of the aforementioned "Star-crossed" piece. To this day, I am still not an expert at Greek mythology but any references are researched to be as accurate as possible.

Radiant

This poem was originally in a caption I wrote for an Instagram post. The smile described belonged to my best friend's little brother, JJ Dantay.

Cosmos (After Ann Druyan)

This poem's last line is in reference to Ann Druyan's love note after the death of her husband — the astronomer Carl Sagan. Carl Sagan's famous line, "Somewhere, something incredible is waiting to be known" also served as the last line for the "Star-crossed" piece.

Dazzling

This poem is inspired by Gabe Bondoc's song "Jacob's Blues" which is about the story of a werewolf and a vampire in a love triangle with a human. You may know this story. It was also a handwritten note in high school that was instantly crumpled up and never delivered.

More Alternatives to the Word "Bae" (After Rudy Francisco)
This poem is directly inspired by Rudy Francisco's "Alternatives to 'Bae'" which appears in his book Helium.

Postcard from the Metaphor
This poem was originally titled "When the Metaphor Says 'Enough'" but was changed to bring the book full circle as well as symbolize the growth it has brought me.

This book is also dedicated to the memory of:
JobJohn Tagapan Dantay

Everything about you was light.

In life, people are either loved widely or they are loved deeply
and you were one of the few that was both.

You will be forever missed, JJ.

Acknowledgments

Postcards from My Bedroom would not be possible without the love and support of all the best people in my life. I am forever grateful for you all.

Thank you to my family: my mother Mariagida Torres; my three amazing older sisters — Mae, Marie, and Bianca; my awesome cousins — David, Joshua, Orion, Patrick, Erika, Kingston, and Princess; and my bonus family — Tita Tess, Jessica Dantay, Genesis Dantay, and Cheryl Parks.

Thank you to my best friends and brothers for always having my back: Joseph Dantay, Ryo Ravelo, Jan Antonio, Jarryd Villacruz, and Robert Baysa.

Thank you to Allison Masikip and Samantha Sobreviñas — I am not who I am today without you both.

Thank you to my teachers who were the first to believe in me and inspired me to one day write a book: Mrs. Rodriguez, Mr. Fazio, Ms. Salinas, Mr. Dominguez, and Ms. Huerta. You may now tell all your students you can see the future.

Thank you to Triveshni Sharma – for always being my biggest fan from the absolute beginning of this all the way from Fiji. Your friendship is the greatest gift I have received from this creative journey. I will never forget you for choosing to come along.

Thank you to Graciela Silva – for always pulling me up the countless times I am down. This book does not exist without your constant reminders and manifestations of its existence. You are proof of the things you can make happen just by willing it.

Thank you to my friends Vikki Wieck, Liza Fernanda Quinn Reyes, Emma Sadlowski, Chanelle Dayrit, Julia Giulietti, Micaela Beaumont, and Neira Lojić for supporting me from all over the world. Thank you all for staying in touch despite our physical distance.

Thank you to my friends Nico Enciso, Agnes Ortaleza, Ashley Masa, Ryan Rodriguez, Abigail Vinas, Michael White, Christine Perez, and Rachelle Rosano as well as Mark Sales, Mary Kim, Gregory Garcia, Marianne Zimmer, and Janet Consolver. I am endlessly thankful to experience a life with you all in it.

Special thank you to Leslie Alejandro and FAHMPortraits for the headshot.

Special thank you to my editor and friend, Vivian Bravo, for always being full of answers when I am nothing but questions. You are truly a gift.

Lastly, special thank you to Sarah Beaudin for designing my book and all of your help; I am beyond grateful.

About the Poet

John Mamaril is a Filipino-American writer from San Diego, California born in 1994. He currently resides in Orange County where he works at the Disneyland Resort for the The Walt Disney Company. He enjoys surfing, playing guitar, and basketball. His favorite creative inspirations and influences include the singer-songwriter Gabe Bondoc, writer John Green, and slam poet Rudy Francisco. He aspires to be just like Michael B. Jordan. He would like to be remembered most for being kind and funny. But mostly kind.